Busy Days

Carolyn Farr   Jane Hutchison

Carol McGrail   Carol Pawlowski

gagelearning

Bias Consultant: Margaret Hoogeven

Writing Team
Carolyn Farr
Jane Hutchison
Carol McGrail
Carol Pawlowski

Editorial Team
Gage Editorial
Joe Banel
Elizabeth Long
Darleen Rotozinski

First Folio Editorial
Fran Cohen
Jane McWhinney
Alison Reid
Tara Steele

Gage Production
Anna Kress
Bev Crann

Design, Art Direction & Electronic Assembly
Pronk&Associates/David Montle

Acknowledgments
Every reasonable effort has been made to trace ownership of copyrighted material. Information that would enable the publisher to correct any reference or credit in future editions would be appreciated.

Photo Credits
12 above Glenn M. Oliver/Visuals Unlimited; below Derrik Ditchburn/Visuals Unlimited; **13** Leonard Lee Rue III/Visuals Unlimited; **14** Michael Quinton/National Geographic Image Collection **15** Breck P. Kent/Animals Animals; **26-29, 37, 68-69** Dave Starrett; **64 upper left** CORBIS, **upper right** V. Last/Geographical Visual Aids, **middle right** Robert Semeniuk/First Light, **bottom** Artbase Inc.; **65 upper left, upper right** Artbase Inc., **middle left** V. Last/Geographical Visual Aids, **lower right** Stephen Homer/First Light; **66, centre** Scott Camazine/Photo Researchers, **upper right, bottom right** Richard C. Walters/Visuals Unlimited

Canadian Cataloguing in Publication Data

Main entry under title:

Gage cornerstones : busy days

ISBN 0-7715-1236-8

1. Readers (Primary). I. Farr, Carolyn
II. Martchenko, Michael
III. Title: Busy days.
IV. Title: Cornerstones: busy days.

PE1119.G23 1999b   428.6   C99-931244-8

Illustrations
4-5 Kim Lafave; **6-11, 18-25, 30-35, 52-55, 76-83** Michael Martchenko; **16-17** Bernadette Lau; **36** Scot Ritchie; **48-51** Margaret Hathaway; **56-63** Barbara Spurll; **68** Anne Stanley; **84-85** Steve Attoe; **96** Philippe Béha; **Cover Illustration** Luc Melanson

Visit our new Web site at www.gagelearning.com

Advisory Team
Jane Abernethy, Chipman & Fredericton SD, NB

Gwen Bartnik, Vancouver SB, BC

Susan Boehnke, Durham DSB, ON

Lisa Bond, Catholic Independent Schools of
  Vancouver Archdiocese, BC

Marg Craig, Lambton-Kent DSB, ON

Laurel Galt, Durham DSB, ON

Gloria Gustafson, Coquitlam DSB, BC

Lise Hawkins, Toronto DSB, ON

Sharon Kinakin, Langley SD #35, BC

Jane Koberstein, Mission DSB, BC

Irene Kovats, Calgary CSSB, AB

Rosemary Lloyd, Durham DSB, ON

Martin MacDonald, Strait Regional SB, NS

Sharon Morris, Toronto CDSB, ON

Cheryl Norman, Delta SD #37, BC

Jennifer Pinches, Calgary CSD, AB

Joanne Pizzuto, Windsor DSB, ON

Pearl Reimer, Edmonton PSB, AB

Maureen Rodniski, Winnipeg SD, MB

Patricia Rooney, Wellington County CDSB, ON

Barbara Rushton, Annapolis Valley Regional SB, NS

Lynn Strangway, Simcoe DSB, ON

Anna Totten, Toronto CDSB, ON

Doreen M. Valverde, Southwest Regional SB, NS

Suzanne Witkin, Toronto DSB, ON

ISBN-13: 978-0-7715-1236-0
ISBN-10: 0-7715-1236-8
3 4 5 6 13 12 11 10
Printed and bound in Canada.

Table of Contents

All selections written by Carolyn Farr, Jane Hutchison,
Carol McGrail, and Carol Pawlowski, unless otherwise noted.

The Best School

There are big schools and small schools
And schools in the middle.
All kinds of schools
For kids big and little.

Schools that have classrooms,
Bells, books, and balls.
Schools that have playgrounds,
Gyms, and wide halls.

Schools that have teachers
And children like you.
But there's no school like our school
Don't you think so too?

Something in the Sky

"Look up there," called Raj.

"Wow!" said the children.

"I can see a big V," said Kim.

"Look at it go! The V can fly," said Ted.

"Miss Day, Miss Day," cried Kim.

"Look!"

"Look at the big V!"

"You are looking at geese," said Miss Day.

"Geese go south, just like the robins.

Geese fly in a big V."

"Can they fly in a ● ?" *circle* laughed Raj.

"Can they fly in a ▲ ?" laughed Dan.

"Can they fly in a ▬ ?" *rectangle* laughed Anna.

"Can they fly in a **K**?" asked Kim.

"Can they fly in a ■ ?" laughed Ted. *square*

10

"What about a heart?" laughed Kim.

"I love hearts!"

The Canada Goose

The mother goose builds the nest.

She lays three to eight eggs.

The father is called a gander.

He keeps the nest safe.

A baby goose is called a gosling.

egg tooth

It has a special tooth on its beak.
It is called an egg tooth.

This egg tooth helps the gosling
to get out of the egg.

Canada Geese

Honkers honking,
Wings wide spread,
V formation,
Lead goose ahead.

Swooping down,
They stop to eat,
Corn and grain,
A tasty treat.

When they're tired,
They come to rest,
Their heads tucked closely
To their breast.

So when the geese
Fly south, just say
Hello to fall,
And the cool crisp day.

Missing

"Where is Hamilton Hamster?"
asked Dan. "He is not in his cage."

"Dan's pet is missing!" called Bud.

"Look! The little door is open," said Anna.

"Tell Miss Day," said Ted.

Raj went to tell Miss Day.

"Hamilton is missing, Miss Day," said Raj.

"Children, let's look for the hamster,"
said Miss Day.

They looked everywhere.

They looked under the table.

They looked on the shelf.

They looked on Miss Day's desk.

They looked under Miss Day's desk.

They looked everywhere, but he was not there.

Bud saw his book bag move.

"Look at my bag," called Bud.

"Look at it move!"

Everyone came to look.

They looked in the bag.

"Here is Dan's hamster," said Bud.

"Oh, look! He has babies!"

"One, two, three, four, five baby hamsters!" said Dan.

Miss Day laughed.

"He's a she!" she said.

Taking Care of a Hamster

A Good Home

A wire cage makes a good home for a hamster.

Put wood shavings on the bottom. Add soft paper for the hamster's bed.

Keep your hamster's home clean.

Good Food

A hamster needs good food just as you do.

It needs
vegetables,

fruit,

and other things.

Give it
fresh water
every day.

Play Time

A hamster sleeps in the day
and plays at night.

Fitness Fun

A hamster needs
lots of exercise.

A treadmill and
a ball are fun.

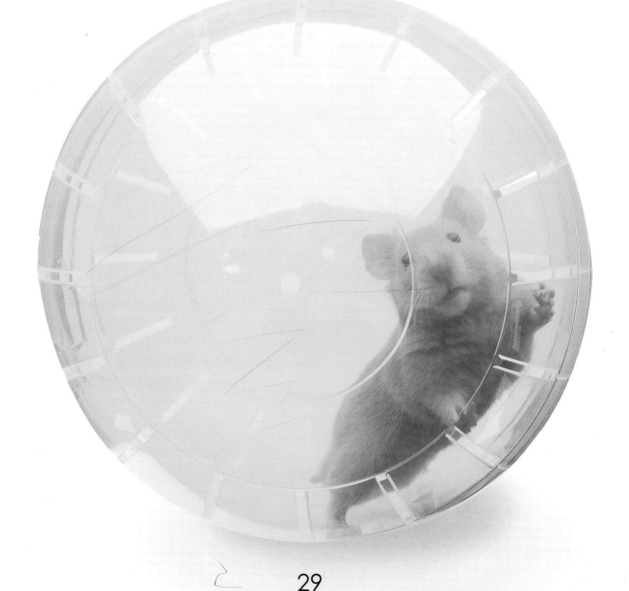

Gym Surprise

"Boys and girls, it is time for gym," said
Mr. Parks.

"Today we will do something new."

Hoops

Parachute

Climbers

Floor Hockey

31

"I am going to play music.

We are going to dance," said Mr. Parks.

"I do not like to dance," said Bud.

"Can we do something else?"

"You may dance
with us when
you want, Bud,"
said Mr. Parks.

The children had fun.

They danced and danced and danced.

Bud saw the children dance.

He saw them having fun.

The children did the Bunny Hop.

The children did the Hokey Pokey.

Then the children got in a line.

They did a Line Dance.

Guess who had the most fun of all?

Dancing Numbers

One, two,
Dance for you.

Three, four,
Tap the floor.

Five, six,
Do twirls and kicks.

Seven, eight,
This is great!

Nine, ten—start again!

All the numbers get in line.
They dance and keep the beat just fine.

Can you line dance?

If Animals Came to School

by Kimberlee Graves

pictures by Karl Edwards

If animals came to school,
it might be hard.

But it might be fun!

If monkeys came to school,
art time would be hard.

But play time would be fun!

If elephants came to school,
story time would be hard.

But getting in line would be fun!

If alligators came to school,
lunch time would be hard.

But field trips would be fun!

If turtles came to school,
some games would be hard.

But some games would be fun!

If camels came to school,
going to the library would be hard.

But coming back from the library
would be fun!

If kangaroos came to school,
music time would be hard.

But clean-up time would be fun!

Do animals come to your school?

Sometimes they come to mine!

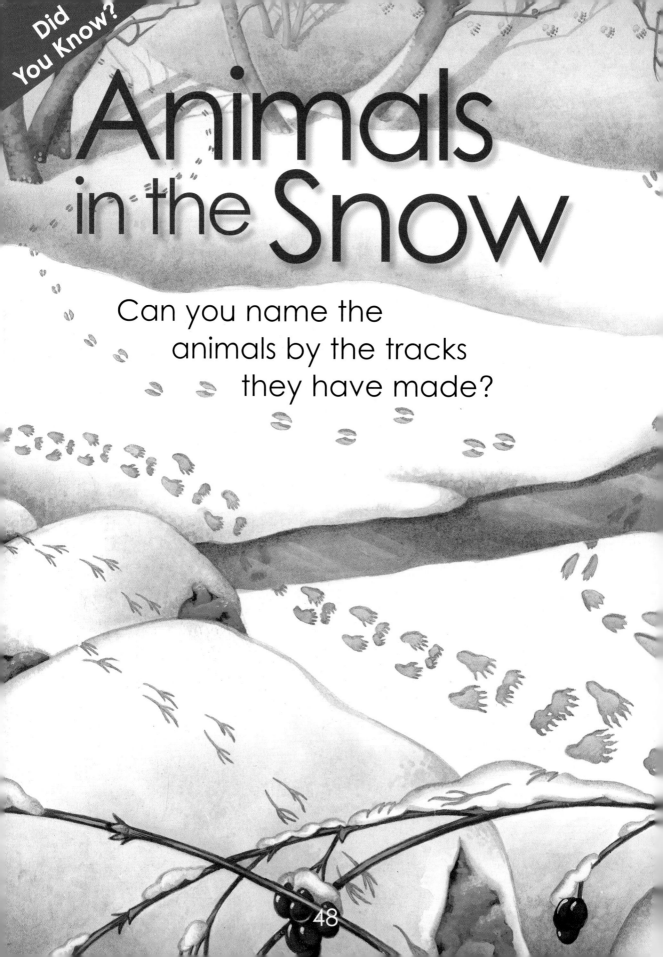

Animals in the Snow

Can you name the
animals by the tracks
they have made?

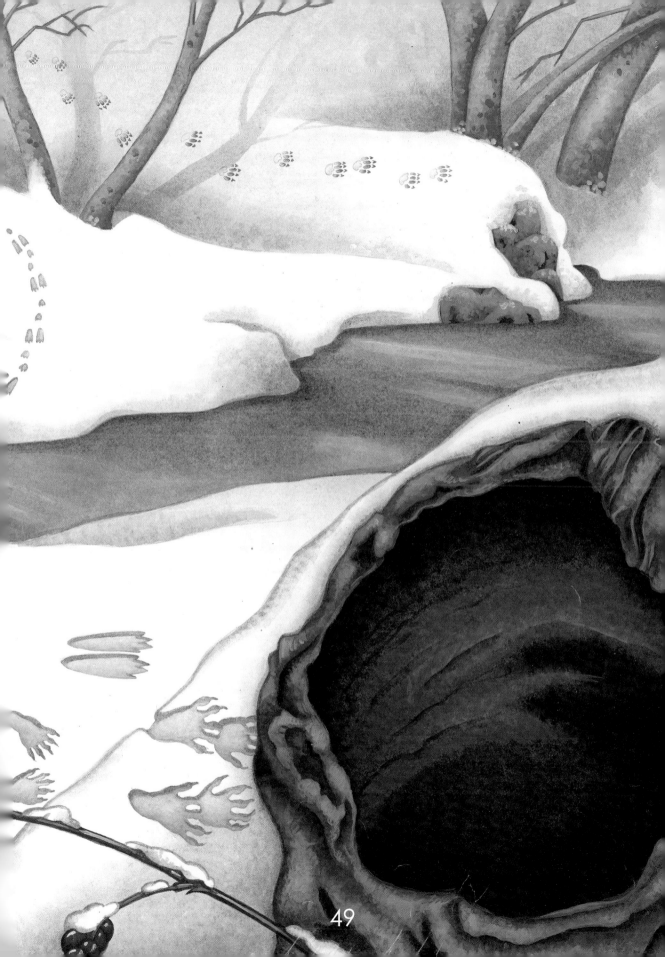

Deer

Chickadee

Wolf

Find out more about these animals.

Snowshoe
rabbit

Raccoon

Snow Party

"Wow! Look at all the snow!" called Ted.

"Let's make a **big**, **big** snowman!" said Dan.

Soon all the children were playing
in the snow.

Miss Day laughed. "It looks like a snow
party!"

The **Biggest** Snowball in the World

"I can make a snowball," said the raccoon.

He began to roll a snowball.
Roll, roll, roll.

"I can help," said the chipmunk.

Roll, roll, roll.

"I can help," said the snowshoe rabbit.

Roll, roll, roll.

"I can help," said the eagle.

Roll, roll, roll.

"I can help," said the wolf.

Roll, roll, roll.

"I can help," said the longhorn sheep.

Roll, roll, roll.

"I can help," said the polar bear.

Roll, roll, roll.

They rolled and rolled the snowball.
It got bigger and bigger.

"Look at that snowball," called the
eagle.

"It's a **big** snowball," said the
polar bear.

It's the **biggest** snowball in the world!" said the sheep.

"What a team!" said the raccoon.

A Canadian Winter

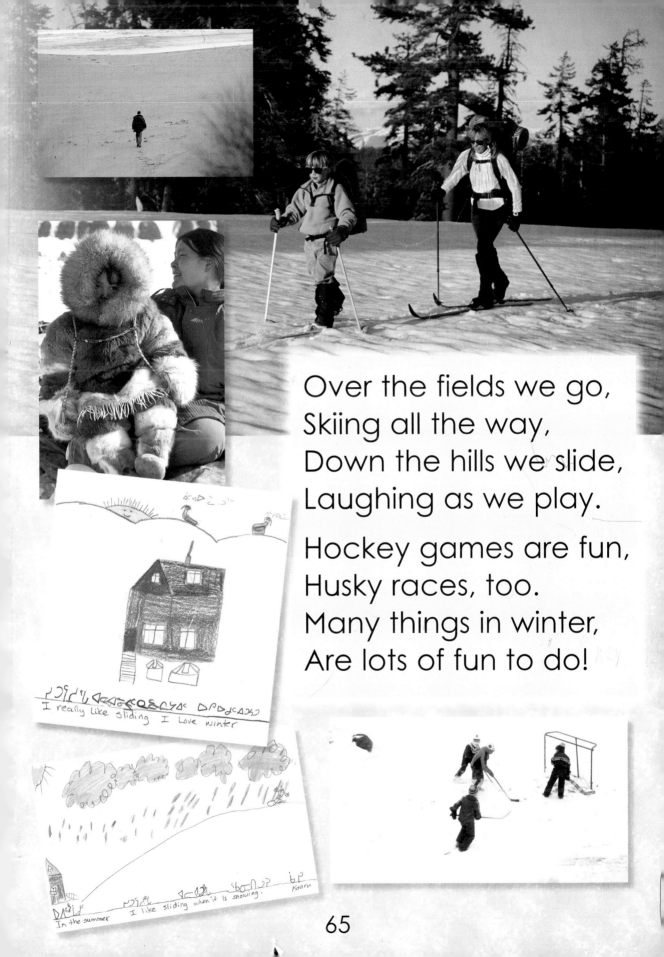

Over the fields we go,
Skiing all the way,
Down the hills we slide,
Laughing as we play.

Hockey games are fun,
Husky races, too.
Many things in winter,
Are lots of fun to do!

ᑐᖓᕕᒃ ᐊᒃᑲᕐᓂᖃᕐᓯᒪᔪᑦ ᐅᐱᒍᓱᒃᑲᓗ
I really like sliding I love winter

ᐅᑭᐊᒃᓯᒃᑯᑦ   ᐱᕐᔪᐊᖅ   ᐃᓄᒃᑎᑑᖅ   ᑲᖐ
In the summer   I like sliding when it is snowing.   Kaaru

Catch a Snowflake

Every snowflake is different.

Some may look alike but no two snowflakes are the same.

Is this true?

Look for yourself!

66

Catching Snowflakes

You will need: a snowy day

a piece of black paper

a magnifying glass

first

1 Dress warmly.

Next

2 Take the black paper outside. Let some snowflakes land on it.

Then

3 Use your magnifying glass to look at the snowflakes on your paper.

finally

4 Draw a picture of the snowflakes.

Make Your Own Snowflake

You will need:

* ❄ white paper   ❄ scissors
* ❄ a pencil   ❄ a round shape to trace

first

1 Trace the round shape on your paper.

Next

2 Cut out the round shape. It is a circle.

Then

3 Fold the circle in half.

After that

4 Fold it into three equal pie shapes.

Next

5 Hold the point and cut pieces out of the sides and top.

Finally

6 Open it up and you will have a snowflake surprise.

Millions of Snowflakes

(poem)

by Mary McKenna Siddals   Pictures by Elizabeth Sayles

One little *stanza*
snowflake
falls on my nose.

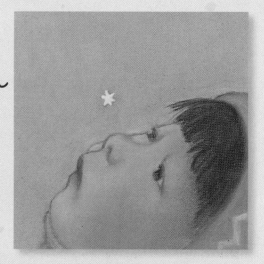

It makes me shiver
from my head to
my toes.

Two little
snowflakes
get in my eyes. *rhyming words*

Blink! Blink!
What a surprise!

Three little
snowflakes
melt on my
tongue.

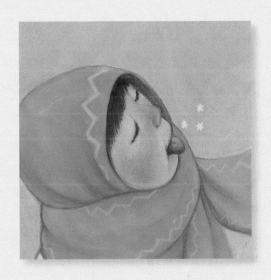

I eat them up.
Yum! Yum! Yum!

Four little
snowflakes
tickle my chin.

I laugh.

I jump.

I run.

I spin. *rhying words*

I stop, and I put out my hand.

Five little snowflakes softly land. *rhying words*

73

Snow on the house.

Snow on the tree.

Snow on the ground.

Snow on me!

rhy ing words (handwritten)

Millions of snowflakes
in my hair.
Snowflakes falling
everywhere!

rhy ing ~~wordig~~ words (handwritten)

Ted's New Look

"Ted, your mother is at the Lost and Found again," called Kim.

"I know," said Ted.

"Why?" asked Kim.

"I lost another mitten," said Ted.

It was time to go home.

Ted went home with his mother.

"Ted," said his <u>mother</u>,

"you have lost six mittens.

No more new mittens for you."

Ted and his mother looked at all his mittens.

There was one red mitten.

There was one orange mitten.

There was one yellow mitten.

There was one green mitten.

There was one blue mitten.

There was one purple mitten.

"Look, Mom. It's a rainbow.

It's a rainbow of mittens!"

The next day Ted came to school.

He was very happy.

"Hi, Robin. I have a new look," said Ted.

Robin looked. "You have one red mitten on and one blue mitten on," said Robin.

"Yes. Cool, eh?" said Ted.

The next day all the children came
to school with the new look.

Lost and Found

I lost my brand new mitten
So I went to the Lost and Found.
I took out all the clothing
And put it on the ground.

I found 8 worn-out running shoes,
And 97 socks,
And more than 50 mittens,
All stuffed in one small box.

There were gym shorts and ski hats,
Jackets, boots, and shirts,
Lunch bags and backpacks,
Ribbons, pins, and skirts.

Lots and lots of mittens,
But my mitten wasn't there.
But, hey! I found my missing glove;
That will make a pair.

It did not smell too pleasant,
I had to hold my nose.
I guess I'll have to wash it,
And soon, before it snows.

Brown Bear, Snow Bear

by Joyce Dunbar   pictures by Kay Widdowson

It was cold. It was starting to snow.

Toby walked Brown Bear 'round the garden.

"Do you like the snow, Brown Bear?" asked Toby.

"It's getting dark and I must go inside. But you can stay outside, Brown Bear. You can stay and watch the snow."

All night long, the snow fell while the moon looked on.

In the morning, the garden was white.

Even before breakfast, Toby went looking for Brown Bear.

But he couldn't see him. Instead, in the place where Toby had left him, there was a soft, white snow bear.

"Hello, Snow Bear," said Toby. "Have you seen Brown Bear? He has ears exactly like yours."

But the snow bear didn't answer.

The snow bear had no eyes.

Toby made him some eyes. He poked two tiny holes in the snow face. Two brown eyes appeared.

"Have you seen Brown Bear?" asked
Toby. "He has eyes exactly like yours."

But the snow bear didn't answer.

The snow bear had no mouth. Toby made him a mouth. He smudged in a mouth and a nose. A wet black nose appeared.

"Are you sure you haven't seen Brown Bear?" asked Toby. "He has a black nose just like yours."

But the snow bear didn't answer.

Instead, he held out his paws. "Shall we make friends, Snow Bear?" asked Toby. "I'm sure you would like Brown Bear. He has paws exactly like yours."

And Toby shook the snow bear's paws. Two brown paws appeared.

"Would you like breakfast, Snow Bear?" asked Toby. "I'm sure Brown Bear wouldn't mind."

Then he lifted up the snow bear. There was a little flurry of snow fur. A cold brown bear appeared.

"Hello, Brown Bear," said Toby. "Have you seen Snow Bear?"